Trick
of the Light

Poems from the life of
Claire Shelton-Jones

edited by Tim Shelton-Jones

Editor: Tim Shelton-Jones

Book design and artwork : Tim Shelton-Jones

ISBN: 9798550370766

Printed by: Kindle Direct Publishing

First Edition June 2021

Published in Great Britain by SJ Books

The cover design includes
the handwritten version of Claire's poem 'Deckchair'.

To the memory of Claire Shelton-Jones
1st April 1952 — 14th March 2020

"We are God's work of art," St. Paul.
(read out in our church on Claire's first anniversary, 14ᵗʰ March 2021)

Thanks and Charities

May I take this opportunity, on behalf of myself and our children Katie and Matthew, and indeed of Claire in her absence, to say a big 'Thank You' to all of Claire's extended family and friends. Your friendship, and your concern for Claire's welfare when her health failed, meant so much to her, and to us, her immediate family.

This book is one way we can all say a big 'Thank You' to Claire in return, as we discover again the pleasure of living alongside her words and thoughts. The Claire we knew and loved will come back to us as we read.

All proceeds from sales of this book will be donated to these charities:
   Uganda Hands for Hope   (https://www.ugandahandsforhope.org)
   Leukaemia and Myeloma Research UK   (https://lmruk.org)

Claire regularly held quizzes and sales in our church hall to raise funds for Uganda Hands for Hope. As you can see from their donations page, *"Uganda Hands for Hope is recognized as a Vetted Organization and a Top-Ranked Organization by Global Giving, a global platform connecting donors with world-changing non-profits".* **Do please feel free to make additional donations to either charity.**

I would not care to write my epitaph.
I only know the sort I would not want:
'She did the washing-up before she went.'

Claire, 7th February 2000

Contents

Introduction

Many who open this book will have some familiarity with Claire's poems. Nevertheless, the scope and intensity of feeling held within these pages will surely come as a surprise and a joy – and sometimes, maybe, a bit of a shock. Her words speak so eloquently of everything in this life that had meaning for her. Here are her hopes and fears, her laughter at little things, her memories of childhood and growing up, her observations of life and her joy in love and nature: Claire's questions and passion flow easily through us, torrents of thought and feeling sometimes calm, often turbulent, always warm and humane. Through her poetry, we begin to see Claire again, with new depth and more completely than any painted portrait or character sketch could tell.

There is so much one could say about Claire. She was an avid reader as well as a witty and prolific writer of poetry, short stories, reminiscences, journals, and entries for the Mass Observation project. Her poem 'And the Girls Made Jam' was published in Smith's Knoll poetry magazine. For fifteen years she ran a highly successful women's writing group in our home town of Brighton. All this on top of working for many years as a teaching assistant with adults with learning difficulties at the Friends' Centre and at City College; doing voluntary work such as taking library books to the housebound; and raising funds for good causes by devising and chairing twice-yearly quizzes at our local Catholic church. And of course her many friends, and her family near, far and departed, meant so much to her, as she to them. And then there was all the housework which the rest of the family didn't do (ie. most of it). But despite this busy schedule, the two of us enjoyed very many happy hours together. I am forever in Claire's debt in so many ways, but then I hope and believe she felt the same about me.

As is so often the case, there are things one discovers and understands about a person only after they are gone. Claire and I did not read that much of each other's written work, but, from what I had seen, I knew she had an exceptional talent for expressing herself in words, and a truly original voice. What I didn't know was just how much written material she had produced – I was astonished to discover well over 400 poems on her computer. Wondering how to break into this hoard, I sorted them in alphabetical order of title, and, proceeding down the list, selected the first 100 or so that Claire herself might have chosen. Many files contained several poems, so there are maybe 500 poems in all (plus earlier ones never committed to digital). All you have here though, in this little book, is a modest selection from her poetic A to Z.

I was tempted to include one or two of my own poems, some of which relate happy thoughts and memories of Claire. But I decided against it, as the purpose of this book is to allow the reader to enter Claire's world of experience, feeling and art, without distraction and in the most direct way possible. So the book is Claire's. And the poems are, as she intended, her gift to family and friends: I know this because she says it herself, in her writing.

So it is time to hand you back to Claire. She was such fun to be with, and now, thanks to the miracle of the printed word and Claire's own powers of invention, here she is again, as full of fun, thought and humanity as ever. I wish you all the joy of a fascinating read, albeit tinged inevitably with great sadness. But the happy memories live on in a time of their own, beyond all harm and forever.

Tim, March 2021

Remembering

I remember the tastes and the smells of my babyhood:
green steaming purée and thick clinic orange juice,
cod liver oil that I promptly spat out,
thick treacly malt that clung tight to the spoon,
junior aspirin disguised in the lemon curd,
making me retch with the shock of deceit.

Parents weren't perfect it seemed: they told lies
about nocturnal visits from fairies or Santa.
I pleaded with Daddy to please never die
but he wouldn't promise: I couldn't see why.

I remember my school with its door in the wall
to a world of strange faces and dead dried-out dinners,
learning my letters on raised bits of cardboard,
scratching with pens dipped in cold china inkwells,
reading out loud from a book titled 'Jackanapes',
hit with a ruler on trembling knuckles
for passing a note round: a joke about teacher,
wetting myself whilst engrossed in a film show,
forced to bring daily some spare, thick brown knickers,
wrapped in a shy paper bag in my satchel.

I remember string shopping bags, baskets on wheels,
sawdust on butcher's floor, farthings and halfpennies,
rides on a trolley bus, 'Listen With Mother',
steam trains and gramophones, black and white telly.

Such cosy trappings blend into the background
of those convent schooldays with black penguin nuns:
not waddling but gliding on unseen smooth castors,
force-feeding guilt of original sin
to a Catholic girl in a captive blue tunic.

23.5.00 (revised 11.6.19)

Friends 1

Separate from family,
sheer pleasure,
guilt free.

Name on a letter,
phone gossip,
best mate.

Handy with tissues,
tear-stained
or giggly.

Always there for you
but knowing
when not to be.

Friends 2

Being a true friend
can take just a moment
or extend beyond a lifetime.
Share your thoughts and dreams
together on the journey.
If you drift apart
blame it on the tide.

14.3.01

The Cemetery Cat

sidles up to us as we walk among the memorials,
stretches out on a shiny marble tombstone
languorously, black on black.

On my father's grave
we plant white and red roses,
arranging them in a tender embrace.
My mother who lay down before him,
will love the roses.

It's hard to picture your parents,
piled one on top of the other,
a layer cake of everlasting love.
Did my mother sigh with satisfaction
when my father finally joined her,
completing their plans?

Or do they both look down from
a higher place,
watching our gardening efforts
with tolerant smiles?

We take photographs,
casting long shadows
in the winter sunshine.

The cemetery cat escorts us out,
past other deceased members of my family
then three poignant babies' tombs
and a plot adorned with photos
of dogs and a miniature
ping pong table
to keep the corpses amused.

At the gate the cat leaves us
and pads back to the residents,
more at home with the dead
than the living.

Return to Osterley

Osterley has coped without me
these thirty years.
Now I return like a ghost
to haunt the park.
There are the trees where I played out
the days of my childhood,
darting through skirts
made of leafy branches.
Inside our secret world I played house,
sweeping my territory clean
with a broom made of twigs.
Passing the two redbrick houses where we lived
I feel like an alien,
walking in streets that are strange
while they still look familiar.
I wonder if I could have dreamed
that I lived here.
The semi I knew had a gate,
front path and neat flowerbeds
but this one pretends with a drive
made of bald and blank stones,
edged with an odd bit of wall,
orange, shiny like plastic.
Doesn't it know that I lived here
from age five to twelve?
How could that room there not care
that it once was our playroom?

Away, a few streets,
to the home where I spent all my teens,
living detached in some style
behind white farm gates.
An oak-panelled hall
led to many large rooms I loved…
Winking at me are familiar
lead-paned front windows.
Making me wince: the front door
white with nasty glass bulges,
the drive full of cars and the
fossil remains of our gates.
Just the old hinges survive
to prove we once lived there.
I stand and cry for a moment
remembering the past.   15.7.02

To My Uncle

I never really knew you till you'd died.
The cosy, genial family man I met
At parties, christenings, weddings, festivals,
Was a façade I never looked behind.
We'd chat a bit, of children, church or work.
You had my father's warmth and sense of fun,
Loving a joke or cheerful anecdote.
Sincere, religious but perhaps less deep?
I thought you had a less enquiring mind
More satisfied perhaps with friendly chat
Than serious discussion or debate.
I never pictured you as deep in thought,
Creative or emotional at heart.

Now you are dead I'll never have the chance
To try and pin you down on things of worth
But I have heard you speak again to me
With such a voice! Words I'd never heard.
My father showed me diaries that you wrote
Year after year, thick volumes packed with thoughts,
Inscribed in flawless, flowing copperplate
Deep thoughts and observations on your life.
Once you had planned a novel. Did you start?...
Give it a shape or was it left unborn?...
Without a chance to grow and live and breathe?

Like me you sent an article or more
To magazines which thanked you for your time,
Thanks, but no thanks. Try again if you'd a mind..
You had a mind!; a mind I never grasped.
You married my aunt after a failed romance
Yet it was not the rebound match I'd thought
But fresh, intense and young throughout the years.
Love letters passed between you all that time.
You could not bear to be apart too long -
Until the day you died.

I'm sorry I never knew you till you'd died.
Perhaps one day we'll have a grand debate
And you can tell me what a writer writes..
Beyond the grave.

                                          8.11.95

Journey

Stepping
from
living
to
dying
is
so
easy.

Gently
miss
breath,
settle
into
stillness.

Autumn

Year
dying
in
golden
last
moments,
dripping
regrets.

Darkness
advances
with
chilling
shadowy
certainty.

18.11.06
(2 sonnets of one word per line)

About Water

Water in the salty seas,
in waves that thrill and depths that kill,
flowed from innocent young rivers,
splashed on stones or pined in pools,
rushed down falls or formed small puddles,
never knowing it would reach
a wider world with different rules,
no longer drinkable and fresh
but ocean deep, inscrutable.

Wash a world away with water,
wipe out traces of dark doings,
boil in kettles, wash white corpses,
bathe new babies, blend strong spirits,
chlorinated, oiled or bubbly,
pamper dirt and sweat away.

Tell us what the world is for:
It's for water, nothing more.

17.5.00

By the Sea

I walk by the sea
into memories of childhood
wafted in on scents
of seaweed.

Watching the waves suck soft shingle
into holes like toothless mouths,
recalls my mother's teeth
grinning from a glass on the bedside cabinet,
greeting the day:
days when I ran
with bucket and spade, paper flags
and bright straw hat
to build my seaside fantasies
and watch them
wash away.

19.2.01

After I've Gone

So hard to see the world
still there without me
But of course I would not see….

My fear of death is
that of vertigo,
letting go
of everything familiar
and falling into the dark.

Will there be someone there
to catch me,
to tell me
I've come home?

11.2.07

After David Copperfield

If I acquired a murderous step-papa
Who killed my weak-willed mother by degrees,
Rather than biting through his jugular,
I'd make him die a poisonous disease.
There'd be some deadly nightshade out the back
I'd make sure that his sister shared the snack.

After I got established in the city
I'd take care to avoid the old school friend,
And find a wife a deal more wise and witty
Than Dora who would drive me round the bend.
And as for Agnes: the smug, holy one
I'd make sure that she entered as a nun.

Micawber - hoping something would turn up,
And only talented at making punch,
Could run a wine bar called 'The Warming Cup'.
I'd take my friend - Uriah, there for lunch.
Uriah was a snivelling, scheming creep
He should end up an alcoholic Heep.

Emily: pathetic, ruined, sad,
The dire result of living close confined,
In isolated boat with fisher lad,
I'd send to school to occupy her mind
She wouldn't need to run away in sin
If she were learning Greek or violin.

Now that you've no need to read the book
And bump into those tiresome folk again
May I suggest instead you take a look
At something fit to occupy the brain
Some modern work without the rambling prose:
Sharp and concise - no frills or furbelows.

After Summer Rain

Branches drip
delicate as pegged out lingerie.
Air feels new-laundered,
cleans my face
with warm affectionate strokes.

Puddles smile at me,
as bursts of brilliant sunlight
disperse the greyness,
lift up sodden spirits.

28.8.06

Altered state

Darkness wraps Thursley Common
tight in a blanket.
It is an alien land
where monsters lurk
behind those grey shapes
known in daylight as bushes.

Soft springy substance
- can it be grass? -
dips and rises underfoot.
Distant pin pricks of light
could be will-o-the-wisp,
firebrand, or car. A star smiles.

Feet reach pavement
with a concrete slap,
the shock of streetlight
reintroducing sight.
Steps, no longer light,
are weighed down
by the world again.

28.11.04

And the Girls Made Jam

Vats of it: boiling, bubbling messes
like cauldrons of rich animal blood.
Sinister, syrupy exploding sweetnesses
spitting out blobs on the cringing white stoves
like snarling cats on heat.
Such steaming anarchy threatens the system.
Cool it down, seal sparkling jars in a pantry,
food for the vicar and old ladies,
spread on crumbly scones or toasted teacakes,
filling a sponge in a cake competition.
Jam and Jerusalem, English home cooking,
sweetness and innocence, harmless as Eve.

20.7.00

An Old Letter

Words from 1939....
my uncle's letter to his wife.
Re-discovering it in 2003, he
copies it in biro
as if new
and posts it again:
to my mother.

"I watched the planes take off yesterday,
fifteen of them
and I saw their return…
just two.
I fear with every silent hour
that Reg is lost
but how can I tell her?"

My mother's first husband
- Uncle Don's best friend,
blown up over Germany,
destroyed in an instant
like so many.
Reading it aloud now is
going back in time
as if I could be sharing their loss.

But I never could….

He should not have died.
But if he had not

I could never have lived.   8.3.03

June

Supposedly summer,
branches heavy
with fresh green foliage
tremble in cool winds,
droop against
sulky clouds.

Our anniversary month:
twenty five years ago
we married under skies
grey as these
but it doesn't matter.
We have all the warmth
we need.

2.6.06

Apple (acrostic)

A single bite in

Paradise

Pollutes.

Life is no longer

Eternal

Apple

Eve was the scapegoat

but there were three

in this marriage.

Satan and Adam

set her up between them.

Cursed with a thirst

for knowledge, she knew

there was so much

they weren't telling her.

Satan said it was simple:

the apple held the key.

Just one bite ….

The apple was bitter

with the flavour of hypocrisy

but now she knew

exactly what that meant.   6.3.05

As We Forgive

Forgive us our trespasses as we forgive ...

Bare-chested men blighting sunny streets,
wobbling red beer bellies in our direction.

England footballers prancing round the ball
like bemused ballerinas out of step.

Those who feel an inexplicable need
to put apostrophes in plurals.

Half-peeled bananas flying out of our hands
into the long grass at picnics.

Coffee that leaks on our blouses
during breaks at work.

Teachers who indoctrinated us
with guilt and low self-esteem.

Brothers who died too young, leaving us with
unfinished business and ageing parents.

Mothers who hoped to control beyond the grave,
leaving put-downs echoing in our ears.

Forgive us our trespasses as we forgive...

Those who cannot ...   28.6.10

Demolition

Bulldozer bites a hole
in bricks, chews, spits out.
I think of T-Rex, eating
the way monsters do,
without the benefit
of table manners.

Sweet

Toffee-topped confection,
smarms its way into
my mouth, creamy,
showing off its flavours.
It dissolves in one sugar rush.
Give me more ....

Baby (acrostic)

Blue, unblinking eyes:
Alive, open to possibilities,
Believing in everything.
Youth is the greatest gift.

5.6.05

New Baby

Imagine I have words for this ....
Call it new life.
I came from wet warmth,
dark floating,
heard drumming from the beat
of my mother's heart.

Change was
a violent eruption
into dazzling light.
I had been pulled apart
from my only home:
my mother.
Where was she?
I was alone.

Then faces fastened on me.
Intrusive, alien, probing hands,
cut away my support line,
lifted me, bundled me up
like a parcel.
I let them have it ....
screamed out my rage,
my terror and loss.

Crying worked. It opened up
the milk bar - so good.
Dimly I could see
my mother's face.
I shall suckle till I want
no more. I wonder ....

what happens next?   5.6.05

Baby Dress

Worn once, its cute
white polka dots
peeped out from the navy
like sailor cadets at attention.

A photo shows my daughter
sulking in it, as if
rebelling over what
she had to wear.

Baby dress vanished
from the wardrobe
whilst she grew big enough
to burst the seams.

Years later I find it:
a dusty heap
stuck behind the hot water tank
in sad reproach.

16.10.05

Gail

Her beautiful life was uprooted.
Stress shriveled her follicles.
She woke each morning
choking on hair:
clumps of blonde curls:
keepsakes from a dead past.

Within four weeks
she was bald:
a striking egghead.
She chose not to hide it,
walked out in the street
head shining,
a beacon of defiance.

Her hair may never
grow back.
She cried for its loss.

I feel the hair on my head
its reassuring thickness:
my comfort blanket
against the cold.

11.6.06

Choosing a name

Will she like it?
How can we know it's 'her'?
Have we the right to choose
an identity for her?
Is it a window
to her spirit
or a convenience
that she can change one day
to a Bella or Jessica
with no fuss?
How can we show
how precious this new life is?

Call her Katherine.
One day it will change to Katie
She will know who she is
and it will be 'her'.

25.1.03

Never Again

Her family never had fun more than once.
Seaside equalled sunburnt feet for Dad
and a temper to bring on Mum's migraine.
The day at the swimming baths stinking of chlorine,
all shining and echoey gave them verrucas.

They had a dog before she was born:
the evidence one photo of a blur
nipping at Sis's ankles.
She had to make do
with a doggy hankie:
soft and safe.

7.4.04

Before You Go

Better not to dwell on the event.
Keep busy.
Focus on preparations
or mixed emotions will disrupt the routine …
I know the house will feel
empty after you've gone.

Yesterday it seems you were
only a baby and your need of me was
urgent, so warm and close.

Goodbye will be the hard part.
Once done I'll be all right.

9.9.04

Berlin - 2004

Visiting you for the fifth time
is like seeing an old friend.
We go back a long way, you and I,
since before The Wall.
When I stared at that barrier of hate
with horrified fascination,
I debated with my brother whether
it would fall in our lifetimes.

It did a year later, crumbling
as if made of papier-mâché.
We had been deceived.
Things were not as solid as they seemed.

My brother died nine years later.
I seem to see him everywhere.
He was so happy here.
That man on the train
could be him side-faced:
with the grey hair he never had the
chance to acquire.

But this city has so many ghosts,
tragedies reflected
in the most tranquil of its lakes.

Remember the dead
but do not let them dull
the light of the sun.
Let it warm my face.

I am alive now.

21.8.04

Birthday Cakes and Bus Journeys

Crystal sits on the bus
busy planning a cake
to buy or to bake
for her lad's birthday tea.
She watches a girl
who displays a nose stud
of a vivid snot green.
Or is it a pimple
to clash with the dimple
on that baby's cheek?
Perhaps by next week
she'll decide on the cake:
maybe green monster face
with some smarties for spots.
The six rows of earrings
in that woman's ear
make her long for a peer
at the holes underneath.
Do her ears look like sieves
for draining out gunge?

Could that baby grow up
to be bald once again,
with some 'hard man' tattoos
and a spike in the chin?
Will her cake take a shape?
Should she buy it or bake it?

27.7.99

Blank Page

Blank page - white, untouched,
crisp in its newness, clean and unafraid,
Why worry it with words?

Why confuse with thought
Something which has no needs?
Just leave it there sifting dust.

If I should scratch on it
Stabbing my sharp intrusive pen
I'll only stir up pain

Leave it tidy there
Safe, uncluttered, in ignorance
Of anything I'd have said.

Murder Mystery

The mystery is how Poirot
gets away with it, bobbing about
in a sea of herrings red enough
to make you blush, his ridiculous
moustache unmoved.

He's done it again: rumbled
the New Zealand aunt in disguise …
what a surprise, just in time
to save that pretty girl from the gallows.
She couldn't be guilty with a face like that:
I should have known.

But how did he get the clue
from the rosebush and know
to switch his tea cup in time
to miss the poison? For a moment there
I thought he'd solved his last case
but no such luck.

11.1.04

Cat Woman

I met her when I sold a heap of books
to eager punters at the church bazaar.
Amongst them was a woman ill at ease,
eyes shifting underneath some thick black hair.
She pushed her purchases at me and mewed,
a gentle mew. How everybody stared
hearing the alien sound escape her mouth!
She opened up a holdall and all eyes
were drawn inside as if to seek the cat
curled up in there amongst her motley shopping.

The woman clawed the contents uselessly:
"My purse!", she squealed. "I cannot find my purse!"
The mewing rose in volume as her search
became more desperate. The hall seemed still
as if transfixed with horror at the noise.
"Mew, MEW", she cried. "MEW, MEW! What shall I do?"
I wondered that myself, and felt ashamed
that my embarrassment should be more strong
than genuine concern for her distress.

I wondered if the mewing would go on
to such a pitch that tigers might appear
as if in answer to her summoning call.
I never knew because she found her purse,
paid for her books and left in anti-climax,
with only these lines to prove that she exists.   27.11.01

Bluebells

Chopped into cardboard,
chunks in a jigsaw,
they diminish:
shapeless blurs with no
reference to tell
where they touch the sky,
no texture or smell except
glue and paper pulp.

But that paper was once trees…
I must search for a bluebell wood
where the flowers are understood.

23.3.03

Old Blue China

One day I will find them in the garden:
blue china fragments
waiting to be dug up from the earth like relics
of my long lost happy home.
Blinking at me from grit and grime
will be angels,
chipped cherubs blowing their own trumpets
in that syrupy way they have.
I will not listen to the tune.

I remember that plate too well:
a treasured heirloom that my mother
invested her most brittle emotions in.
In our house things never fell apart.
They were not allowed to.
People who let things slip
were careless and weak.
That was what my father said.
And he never, never broke
a thing.

It was in the bottom layer
of a three tier cake tin.
Cheese straws sat in the top,
waiting for the party.
What was in the middle layer
I forget but
my father picked up just the top.

Two tiers smashed down
on kitchen tiles,
broken angels bursting out
in a shower of bloody jam sponge
and my mother cried.

It broke her heart
but my father said it could have happened to anyone
and who ever heard of a three tier cake tin?
The plate was glued and held together with rubber bands
in a crude parody of its former self.
One day when I have to dispose of such things
I will burst the fault lines
and bury the shards
until resurrection day.

9.5.00

Anniversary

The third anniversary of my brother's death
caused me to wonder, as I had before,
how best to mark it, and what he would have thought,
and if there are ever people with the courage
to ask such questions of their dying loved ones.
I hated the outings of the last two years,
the driving with my tense and aged parents
to see his memorial and stand forlorn
shivering in the cold November air.

This year my father was not well enough
to make the trip and so I went alone,
deciding to walk, a 40 minute trek
feeling the freedom of the morning air.
Perhaps it was a pilgrimage of sorts
not to a saint but just to pay respects
to someone who was once so much alive.
I took with me two bunches of pink roses
made out of silk; but 'planted' in the rose bush
they looked quite real. I said a silent prayer
then feeling I had done what should be done,
got on a bus, so glad to be with people.
Sipping a mug of coffee in a cafe
I wished my brother could be there with me.   27.11.01

Night Out

She puts on her party face,
trembling hands trying to paint
perfection onto adolescent angst.
The face she sees in the mirror
is not one she recognises.
It will gaze through blurred features,
hear loud disconnected sounds,
speak carefully-rehearsed phrases.

Later she will come home,
wipe it off,
smile with tired recognition
and see herself again.

                                        23.3.03

Bodmin Moor

Wild ponies graze on grassland.
Yellow gorse dazzles against sky
unexpectedly, piercingly blue.
We walk in bright sunshine.
Sheep gaze impassive as we skirt mud,
climb steep, high stone stiles,
brush against blossomed branches.

A circle of ancient stones awaits,
story hidden in forgotten mists.
We enter the ring:
See two figures
enacting solemn ritual
with black cauldron and forked stick.
We keep our distance:
afraid to look closely
at deep secrets.

A sense of the sacred remains
in this timeless place.

16.4.09

Bond

The definitive one
was dark, silky smooth,
with a Scottish touch.
Shaken on occasion
but never stirred,
his essential ingredient
was sangfroid.
Blended with women,
the result was sticky.
Who did the clearing up?

30.10.05

Bread

The smell of baking bread,
it is said,
sells houses.
But first of all that glorious smell
sells
bread.

The aroma maddens and
murders restraint.
I bite deep, tearing
the crust like flesh,
reducing substance
to crumbs.

Bread is magicked
by mysterious alchemy
from a raw sticky mess
to food for starving stomachs

and estate agents.

24.7.02

Broken Glass

The day I tripped and dropped the milk :
it burst out of its glass restraint
spurting joyfully in a stream
to splash the cool, compliant tiles.
Glass crumbs twinkled prettily,
in the spreading milky sea.
Flustered I dabbled with the drips,
mopping with a flimsy cloth.
The sparkly bits of glass attacked:
cutting, stinging spitefully.
Red blood spots splashed into the white
to give a strawberry milk effect:
so cheerful-looking that I smiled
in spite of feeling so cut up.

14.12.99

45

Burning Boats

No-one could put on a funeral like the Vikings.
What a show - such style they had!
Instead of wet graveside with mumbling vicar
or cold, conveyor-belt clean crematorium,
they sent a tall ship with fierce dragon prow
on a last fiery journey through deep, doleful waters
over the dark horizon to another world.
The soul of the proud warrior
cleansed and freed by flame,
flew to Valhalla - straight as an arrow.

You too can burn your boats.
Be free and re-born, unburdened by memory.
Leave the land and your baggage behind.
Step on the boat without looking back.
But don't cry when you go
or you'll make the sails wet
and the matches won't catch.

20.7.00

November 1st 1999

November is a drippy, sticky time
of piled-up sodden leaves forming a sludge
like mushy golden cornflakes in a bowl.
I fetch the milk to wash the cereal down
in from the doorstep, squashing a catalogue
of Christmas orders: colourful sheets of stodge
depicted - from meat pies to chocolate treats,
millennium biscuit tins and fizzy pop.
Prising a leaflet from reluctant bottles,
I find they've left a milky circular mark
prominent on the cover, and the stain
stands out in symmetry - a perfect wheel,
replica of the Giant Millennium wheel !
Is this an omen of millennial doom?
There will be many more absurd than this
before the century settles down to die,
not with a bang or whimper but a sigh
of past regrets and future trepidation.
Meanwhile we have November to survive,
a month of many deaths from saints to souls.
And Halloween howls from children at the door,
demanding treats and holding out their sacks.
A little devil with a bright red face
tries for a second round of chocolate bar
but I refuse him and he grins at me.
We understand each other. We must try
to get away with everything we can,
before it's all too late and nothing's left.

2.11.99

47

The Stranger's House

The stranger's house that I visit in dreams
is a place for exploring rooms within rooms,
leading to mazes of passages piled
with parcelled-up ideas, memories, crates full of childhood.
Discarded toys tease at locked-away memories,
dressing up boxes conceal many games,
acres of books suggest treats to be tasted
but cannot be opened, sealed tight like hard wax.

I'm sometimes alone but often with people,
who drift in unbidden from past and from present.
The ones who have died sit and talk to me calmly
of life after death as a serious business.
They look at me sadly but leave me quite lightly,
a peaceful dissolving of shadows in silence.
The living seem different, unlike themselves
without the restraints from the world of the waking.
Illogical, flippant, affectionate, angry,
their speech seems to echo like ripples in water.

I rest in a room which is vast, light and airy.

A large high white bed lets me float on it drowsily,

watching the walls which surround it - all glass,

reflecting a pool of cool, rippling currents.

Pre-Raphaelite maidens smile in through the glazing.

I walk out to meet them on bright polished wood.

My bare feet can feel the hard grain from the tree trunks,

grown in a forest of oaks, long since dead.

Further encounters are stopped by my waking,

abrupt interruption - a break in the film.

The house I'm in now seems so solid, familiar

but is it the stranger's or is it my own?

9.11.99

By the Pool

I choked by the pool on lungfuls of chlorine,
pale, disinfected, toes splayed on white tiling,
standing as stiff as a corpse in a cupboard
before the knees lock into true rigour mortis.
Echoing sounds muffled-up by my swim cap,
ears rubber-sealed ripped apart by sharp whistle:
"Six o'clocks jump in!", big splashes all round me -
solitary, stuck there transfixed by the poolside.
Glued to its damp rim and fixed on the blue depths
where far below me, the alien life forms,
stared at me sniggering, leered at me, giggling,
forced me to plunge down to drown in the shallows.
Sticky and slippery, shivering wet me,
reaching for handholds and grabbing a swim float -
white as marshmallow - a plump polystyrene,
I clung to it madly, kicking not moving,
watching the others glide gracefully past me,
reaching the far side and stopping to watch me.

He choked by the pool on lungfuls of outrage,

my swimming instructor: a failed army chief,

bullied me weekly and railed at mc bleakly,

his permanent failure, stubborn non-swimmer.

Tugged at by tow-ropes or buoyed up by giant floats,

flailing with flippers as slimy as kippers,

I stared at the clock and its slow, sluggish hands.

For centuries stuck there, cursed in a nightmare

waiting for magical aid to release me:

"Six o'clocks out please!", the blessed deliverance,

scrambling and slithering out on the poolside,

plodding across to my personal locker,

re-claiming life as I took my belongings.

I choked by the poolside on lungfuls of comfort,

locked in my cubicle, sealed off from danger,

giggling relief with wet, warm, heavy gaspings

fuelled by fresh sound as I tore off my swim cap.

Six days before me, so easy and swim-free ....

until they would make me come back to the pool.

16.11.99

Pains in her head

There was a young woman
with pains in her head
who went to the doctor
but he found instead
that a spider had made
its home in her ear.
It found its way in —
Why it stayed isn't clear.
Perhaps he was warm
and he liked the dark space
feeding on microbes
that lived in the place.
The eardrum is loud,
Did he dance to its beat?
Was he sad when ejected
his life incomplete?
It was in the paper,
no word of a lie.
The doctor reports
that the girl didn't die.
But I want to know
the fate of the spider.
Did it wriggle away?
Had it giggled inside her?

Ghost at the window

I read the book of course,
shared Cathy's passionate journey
through life to a death that brings no peace.
My warm living flesh
shudders to think of hers:
so bitter, cold,
irreversibly dead….

Yes, I know death is final
but why should it have the last word?

I heard the song of course.
worked hard to make out the words
sung by a banshee in torment?
My warm living flesh
aches to comfort her …

Yes, I know death is final
but why should it have the last word?

Yes, I know ……

16.6.03

Forty days in the desert

Christ went on a package tour called 'Desert Meditations'.

Food and drink were not thrown in : strict dietary regulations.

Great for getting suntans but the skin dried out like leather.

No need to take much luggage - you could count upon the
weather.

Mirages available as options for no fee:

views of lakes and fountains, food and wine beneath a tree.

Dreaming has no calories - great weight-loss guaranteed.

You might feel weak but you would be as skinny as a reed.

Forty days and nights went by, the usual peace and quiet,

spiritual reflections and imagined hearty diet.

Then as he was packing, Christ received a strip o gram:

but not a lovely lady more a sleazy-looking man.

He said to call him Satan or Beelzebub would do.

Old friends called him Lucifer, but it was up to you.

Why he had so many names the devil only knew

but as an entertainer he didn't have a clue.

Donning a fetching costume of scaly green and grey,
Satan rubbed his pointed horns and magicked them away.
He took Christ to a field of stones to turn them into bread
but Christ said, like a poet, that he lived on words instead.
Then they climbed the temple to try jumping off the top.
Christ was having none of that and said they'd have to stop.
Satan said: 'Let's bungee jump but leave out the elastic.
Angels will surely catch us and the view should be fantastic.'

Maybe Christ had vertigo - he wouldn't play the game
so Satan said a mountain walk would help to clear his brain.
When they reached the peak and stood to marvel at the view
Satan offered him the world, the stars and heaven too.
'I'm not that way inclined', said Christ. 'I cannot worship you.
Now I think you'd better leave. I have lots of things to do.'
Satan sulked and went to find a more obliging friend.
He had to work on Judas but he won him in the end.

14.2.00

Good Friday

And I draw my eyebrows
to the sound of birdsong.

These Cornish mornings are
so hushed and peaceful:
all demands on me left far behind.

Here the dawn chorus woke me
with its infectious innocent joy.
Dozing off again I dreamed of the past.

So much of the ancient world here:
witches and standing stones,
Celtic crosses and mossy holy wells.

An earlier language lurks behind
the locals' rustic burr, left in the names of
places, draped in the black and white local flag.

The sound of bygone names sifts
the soft air… Saints Petroc, Piran, Kew
and Breward, Issey, and Little Pretherick.

Our moorland walk lacks rain, wind or mist.
Turf springs back dry and crackly underfoot
and the gorse blazes a brilliant sunshine yellow.

High hedges sprinkled with primroses, bluebells,
pink campion, hide the view on winding lanes,
allowing only glimpses of fields and rocky coastline.

Too glorious a day to think of death: the solemn
stripped churches and the cross.
I am alive … every breath a blessing.

                                                        18.4.03

Cameraman

Noah has a camera
to film the drowning earth,
saving many species:
for a film, not a re-birth.
Filming fauns and unicorns,
is he beloved by God?
Or as he snaps each dying breath,
is he a callous sod?
The waves are lapping round the ark,
the cries becoming faint,
the sky is growing slowly dark
above our pseudo saint.
Smugly he puts the camera down,
eyes the chosen few,
wrings the dampness from his gown,
admires the empty view.

1.12.06

Candlelight

I once lit a candle for you.
Its yellow flame burned
with childlike hope
in a vast dark space,
a prayer flickering hesitantly
a tiny way towards Heaven.

Now in the warm candlelight
of family gatherings
I wonder at your absence.

6.3.01

Castles

I'll build a castle of my words:
not one of sifting, shifting sand
squashed by bare feet or drowned by waves.
My edifice will be of stone,
weather-beaten, grey and bleak,
softened by rich crops of moss,
brightened by the rising sun
shining on the secret cracks
where I slide my messages
for a future tourist trail
in a post-poetic age.

If the solid-seeming walls
crumble in the fist of time
to fragments of anarchic thought
still the ruins will retain
memories of what happened there.
But if ages smother them
in annihilating dust,
where will all my fine words go ?
Will they seep into the soil,
to fertilise a future world,
bring forth immortal trecs?

3.5.00

Claire Without Hair

Do I dare to look?
I never expected to see
her bare, scared scalp
pink and perplexed
I look in the mirror at her
Or is it me?
An imposter skulks, sadly
Eyes reproachful
They ask
Where are my curls?
Am I Claire
Without hair?
I stare
At the stranger.
She looks a bit
like my Dad
Definitely one
Of the family.
Must I welcome her?
This new 'me'
Is scary
But is Claire.
Who else
Would it be?
Hallo me!
We must agree
To get on
Until the day
Claire's hair returns
Like a long-lost friend.

6.1.2020

Not Me

Please miss, no miss, it
wasn't me miss, not me.
Someone else must have
begged to be excused, must
have wet their knickers, when
you said not now but it
wasn't me miss, not me.

Please sir, no sir it
wasn't me sir, not me.
Someone else must have
smoked those fags, behind
the bike sheds, burnt Tom's
games kit but it
wasn't me sir not me.

Please Joe, no Joe it
wasn't me Joe, not me.
Someone else must have
said they loved you, broke
your heart when they dumped you
for that sexy Gary but it
wasn't me Joe not me.

Please kids, no kids it
wasn't me kids, not me.
Someone else must have
left you and not sent
your mum the money,
let you think you had no dad
but it wasn't me kids, not me.

Please God, no God it
wasn't me God, not me.
Someone else must have
killed the wildlife, chopped
the trees down, poisoned rivers
bombed civilians but it
wasn't me God not me.

21.1.02

Musical Memories

There were no videos in the 1950's
but I re-wind our childhood melodies.
Four years ahead of me, you set a cracking pace,
main music maker of the family.
First with a broken wind-up gramophone
we giggled over gasped-out melodies
wrung from old 78s like squeezed out socks.
From mangled antique odes we turned to tunes
played on a record player that you earned:
a present for passing your 11 plus.
Mono LPs played jolly Scottish songs,
music accompanying strange new ballet steps,
and classical greats to feed my many moods,
my fear of soldiers marching through the door
summoned by Holst and his 'Mars The God of War'.

We grew up with family sing-songs in the car,
and every Christmas meant relations ranged
around the piano played by willing aunt
belting out hymns and old-time music hall.
Pop songs and jazz accompanied our teenage years
your many romances, my fumbling few.
You chose the Hi-Fi for my twenty first
demanding as always nothing but the best.

Later when you left, the house was quiet
until you came back from your frequent trips,
filling the place with instant startling sound:
your voice, your records turned to maximum.
Over the years you quickened up the pace
developing an ever greater range
of life experience, always playing well
until the final movement went off key.
Dying you made your plans efficiently,
selected music for your funeral.
And so we sat with you, to hear it through.

Where is your music now? I hear the quiet.
I long for one false note but it's all gone …

                                        29.6.99

Christmas 2014

Christmas morning before dawn
The world is hushed, expectant
We drive through the dark, quiet streets
My heart beats

There in the hospital
My daughter in labour takes my hand
Her fingers squeeze mine
As the pains come
Together we travel on a long
Hard journey towards life

The sun rises over the shining sea
The world wakes to Christmas Day
Christ is born again
And this child is also coming
Pushing his way towards the light
He arrives before the sun sets
And the sky again is golden
With blazing joy

As I hold my tiny grandson
In my tired, proud arms
He looks at me
With dark, liquid eyes
And I see eternity.

Changing Church

The roof is sky:
nearer to heaven
than vaulted ceilings
soaring above the heads
of congregations squashed
into awe-struck pews.

The floor is earth,
soft and damp
rather than neat mosaic.
Feet walk on moss
instead of shining brasses
marking important tombs.

The walls are air,
sweet with the scent of flowers
replacing incense.
Birds are the choristers:
their holy song,
echoing ancient voices.

20.5.06

Canterbury Cemetery - 1

This is a place of quiet calm
where breezes gently stir
the leaves of tall green trees.
Rose bushes meet beside the path.
Benches sit thoughtfully in shade.
Slowly he's wheeled…

to his late wife's grave.
The old man rises,
walks a few paces,
leaning hard on his stick.
Briefly he stands and sobs,
shoulders hunched,
then steps across the path
to his parents' plot.

He will not come again:
much as he loved her,
she is not there.

28.7.09

Canterbury Cemetery - 2

This is a place of quiet calm
where breezes gently stir
the leaves of tall green trees.
Rose bushes meet beside the path.
Benches sit thoughtfully in shade.
Gravestones tell stories
to her as she lingers,
putting off the moment off.

At her mother's grave,
the silent stone
tells her so little.

Still she clings on,
trying to help her father:
saying mum's happy now…
and how much she loves him.

Later at lunch
she talks about an aunt,
buried nearby
who died as a young girl.
Nobody marked her grave.

28.7.09

China Doll ,

She has a china face,
chalk white and cold
to the touch.
Blue eyes blink open
when you move her,
look at you with a question.
Straight black hair parted is
stiff as starched curtains,
opening onto the past.

A little girl loved her,
played secret games,
carried her to bed,
hugged her so much that
her fingers and toes
crumbled at the edges.

Today Diana sits primly
on my mother's bed,
propped up by lacy cushions,
waiting…
When I go in the room
she looks at me, says:
"Who are you? You're not the one.
Where has she gone?"

24.6.07

Christmas and Millennium Thoughts

Christmas Eve meant rain and violent winds
unfestive and unfair to travellers,
perhaps anticipating stormy scenes
in many households over seasonal chores:
getting the turkey stuffed, the presents wrapped,
prising the mother-in-law from the kitchen sink
where stubborn rubber gloves like suction pads
stake out her claim to own the territory,
churning out half-washed plates at lightning speed
splashing the soapy water on the floor.

Millennium Eve meant misty, drizzly skies
which could not blur the fireworks and the buzz
anticipating midnight and the start
of some new mystery: a brand new world.
Ecstatic crowds were glad to be alive,
feeling a smugness at their own survival
to see the new year in, new century
and new millennium - a unique chance
to start again with three-fold resolution.
I hate to spoil the pleasure of so many
but is 2000 more than just a name?
Did anyone wake next day not just the same?

5.1.00

Cliff (acrostic)

Chalky

landmark:

innocent,

free,

floating.

Sour (acrostic)

Suck a lemon,

overdose on

undiluted vinegar,

recoil with pursed lips.

16.9.04

Seven Sisters

Tall, pale ladies of distinction,
delicately stretch above pebbles,
try not to bruise dainty toes
on all that roughness.
Forever linked,
they stand and breathe
the salty Sussex air.
Gales lash their faces.
Do they whisper in the dark?

"See our mother the moon,
gives us a night light,
soothes with showers of stars.
But our father the wind
beats us cruelly, sometimes.
Tonight he is gentle
whistling a lullaby.
The seagulls are singing,
nesting in our long white skirts."

Seven sisters smile, teeth gleaming.

16.9.04

Cornish Calm

We stroll on grassy cliff tops

stunned by a sapphire sea

sparkling in sunlight.

King Arthur's Castle looks surprised:

its sharp, rocky ruins

more used to

the roar of tempests lulling its ghosts into slumber.

A skylark sings its heart out,

swoops down to look at us, unafraid.

We cannot capture anything

but the memory of a moment.

10.4.07

The Importance of Colour: a review

In the sixties 'The Forsyte Saga'
was a black and white sensation
but colour was not lacking.
Characters crazed with it
came out of the screen
to chat with you in your living room
over the tea cups.
The aunts gossiped under twittering curls
and the uncles' outrageous whiskers
tickled the pale cheeks of the ladies.
They were callous and classy and rich
but you cared about their fate.
They were people you could have been
in a different age.

In 2002 the new 'Forsyte Saga'
is a colourless costume drama,
filmed in colour, perfectly formed
but without the passion.
The actors seem like frauds
pretending to be the 'real' ones
but fooling nobody who saw the originals.
The aunts are just background scenery,
Soames lacks slime
and Young Jolyon looks so 21st century
when he calls his father 'Dad'.
We've been had.

8.4.02

Couch Potato

Pale as an uncooked chip
he lolls among tired cushions,
one podgy arm holding
the remote control like a magic wand,
the other up to the elbow in a giant
crisp packet. Mesmerized by the screen
the poor creature vegetates,
imprisoned on his couch
like Kafka's giant insect.

1.2.04

Reader, kindly note this is not me! (I'm not even that keen on crisps) — Ed.

Meeting

Was I expected?

Which way do I go?

What's the agenda?

Where are the minutes?

Why am I here then?

Who called the meeting?

When will it be over?

Will there be feedback?

Who's asking questions?

Who wants to know?

1.2.04

Errors

Errors were white once:

bleached by correcting fluid

never quite hidden.

Now it's too easy.

All those deletions

by computer look as if

we've got it right.

The sheet of paper

is a little white lie.

1.2.04

Couples

Five couples meeting for 15 years
pretending it's just to play "Trivial Pursuit",
caring with the lightest touch
and much laughter.
Seeming as solidly wedged together as the plastic "cheeses"
in the wheels awarded for clever answers
on the right squares.

Over coffee and chocolates (the usual prize)
somebody makes an announcement:
"We've often joked about the first couple to get divorced.
Well it's us!"
An habitual gag. His wife laughs with the rest of us but
goes on too long. Laughter in our faces dies as her hysteria
and his agony attack the sudden silence
like a savage knife.
"Never take each other for granted",
he warns as he calls for a whisky.
And his wife laughs on as if she will laugh forever…
too embarrassed to stop.

6.10.02

Traffic Jam

Drivers stewed in the jam
like sweating lumps of fruit
while schoolchildren marched through
the streets demanding an end to war.

Drivers muttered about lost business:
appointments that would not be kept,
while children walking knew that miles away
children would never walk again.

All day the city rang with angry shouts
and a passionate excitement.
We were all as helpless as the stalled traffic
while the blood in Iraq flowed on
and congealed in the hot desert sun.

1.4.03

Garden Party

Invitation only:
my father - a London mayor,
the reason we could go there.
Men wore morning suits:
misnomers in the afternoon.
Women were in pretty frocks,
white gloves and hats.
My dreamy polka dot dress
topped by pink millinery,
matched the flamingos on the lake.
We nibbled minute sandwiches,
sucked on succulent strawberries,
while greater VIPs
were presented.
We can say we have been
to tea with the Queen.

12.7.06

Cross

Cross about finding
nothing in the hole ...
where her mind should be,
she searched for a memory
of anything to write about.

The cross she had to bear
was recalling people
she could never see again.
Regretting lost opportunities,
relationships broken off by death
left jagged, incomplete.

Crossed in love more than once
she'd wept and wailed,
sobbing self-consciously,
composing sickly ditties
to worthless lovers.

A favourite cross she wore
was a Celtic cross
of coloured marble fragments.
A smooth, calm, ornament
rather than the twisted
suffering on the giant crucifix
dominating Catholic childhoods.

Should she cross the bridge between
her past and present
resuscitating dying phrases?
or should she pioneer words
in verses for the future?

Crossing the Channel

People pass over in ships or planes,
tunnel under or even swim it
lathered in grease to keep out the cold.
It is a void between parallel universes.

No-one can join the irreconcilable.
Beyond the midway point is where
all foreignness starts.

Not only do chips become 'pommes frites'.
(My spell-check sees **red** at the thought.)
Everything changes from left to right,
royal to republican, C of E to RC:
at least nominally.

Tony Blair does not rule over there!
Why not cross over and never come back?

12.7.06

Crumble

Squelchy underneath
from juicy cooked fruit,
it sticks to teeth like glue.
The top is like cement
forming an outer dental mould.
Your fangs may crumble.

7.10.04

Sorry (haiku)

I say it often
when someone bumps into me,
smiling stupidly.

7.10.04

Anywhere but here (acrostic)

Ambling along a foreign avenue

noticing unfamiliar architecture

yet still breathing European air, or

whiling away the time in Asia

hoping to drink in

every exotic sight.

Revelling in the otherness of the

east, the smells, dust and

bustle of humanity.

Under desert skies,

travelling by camel

happy not to be there in

England stuck in traffic or

riding a tube train

enduring armpit odours.

7.10.04

Dark Ages

The stars are brilliant diamonds
from a necklace threaded long ago,
scattered across space and time.
The Milky Way is a blur among them,
like a child's chalk fingerprint
on a giant blackboard.   15.10.06

Clouds

I regret the appearance of clouds:
dark grey ones block out the sun.
Pink flushed streaks at sunset
show the dying of the day.
White puffs fly across the sky like woolly sheep,
impossible to hold or stroke.   15.10.06

Book (acrostic)

Breathe in the heady aroma of
Old words written in dust.
Open up the door to
Knowledge of magical worlds.   15.10.06

Dark Night

Girls and boys come out to play
in the dark November night.

The Moon shines among starry sparklers
as people walking in a body
down quiet streets
echo past fanatics intent
on more deadly missions:
hangings? and witch hunts?

What are we part of here?
There is a burning certainly.
Down on the common
Guy Fawkes is set alight again.
We cheer as he expires in a
protracted agony of bangs.
The stars are sulking at their
rivals pirouetting in gaudy costumes
with cheeky whizzing and whirring.
Waterfalls of light have their
brief moments of glory before
vanishing back into the dark.

Crowds disperse,
leaving the moon and stars
to settle back into the comfort
of the silent sky.
The ghost of Guy Fawkes
sighs, is laid to rest
for another year.

10.11.03

Dark

I don't want to know
where you think the candlesticks should go,
who should be taking charge of bits and bobs
after your death.

I don't want to read
your screed about prized collections,
having to keep the cranberry glass complete
like a curator in a 'Museum Of You'.

I don't want to feel
that you'll control me after your life is done,
keeping your terror of the dark at bay
by giving commands today.

I want to know I'll keep the parts of you
revealed when the agenda's set aside:
glimpses of that person you could be,
the one I would grasp before you disappear …

3.2.05

*Claire's footnote: My mother died in 2006 and I am still working through
my feelings but it is getting better…. (September 2012)*

Buttered Toast (acrostic)

Begin with an

Uncooked slice and

Toss it in a

Toaster.

Eventually a

Radical change

Ensures that a

Delicacy will emerge.

The toast that was

Once just

A plain piece of bread

Shows the miracle a touch of

Temperature can achieve.

8.2.05

December (acrostics)

Dark days illuminated by
expectation of
Christmas cheer will
eventually reach the
merry-making time when
bloated party-goers
enjoy the prospect of a
rest from exhausting festivities.

Daft isn't it, that
everyone enjoys
counting the days: the
expectation
mainly;
but finds even more
enjoyable the
remembrance afterwards?

14.12.03

Day Trip

A slow summer dawning
for these early risers,
driving through landscapes
of enduring Englishness:
hazily perfect, ever familiar.

Packed on the ferry boat
processed and rucksacked,
they stake out their territory,
queue for the café,
watch fellow passengers, hear the announcements.

Disgorged on French soil
like limp bits of salad
they're tossed in a dressing
of strange sounds and fragrances,
mixed in with rich food, washed down with cider.

Joined to the Channel
by unseen umbilicus,
stretching their rope
they climb up to the castle,
looking at views of the harbour and seafront.

Slowly pulled back

via churches and shopping streets,

picking up groceries,

trudging with carriers

they're pulled to the ferry by powerful magnets.

A late summer evening

for these tired travellers,

driving through landscapes

of enduring Englishness:

ever familiar as if never left.

6.8.01

Bubble

Floating frivolous, free
for a delicate delicious moment,
catching rainbow colours,
dancing on currents of air,
unaware that a touch is all it takes
to burst your bubble.

14.12.03

Deep Breath

Take it slowly.
Move forward.
Ignore the lookers-on,
the knocking of your knees.
Concentrate. You
can do it. It all begins
with that first deep breath.

14.12.03

Desert Island (acrostic)

Dazzling
endless
sand,
exotic
rare
trees.

I
sit
languid,
alone:
nothing
doing.

27.9.08

Desert Landscape

Reddening ripples of sand dance under dying sun,
bathed in a pool of dark blood.
Hints of coming night are the thin shadows
like slashes in fabric, cut by an unseen hand.

Fitful wind picks up particles of sand, plays
with them in grim imitation of life. This is
an empty stage, its dramas acted out
long ago. All warmth has gone.
Cold and darkness are the final act.

27.2.06

A Woman's Urge to do the Dusting

Would shifting particles of skin and hair
through the air, from one surface to another
achieve anything creative? If I were dusting
instead of writing this poem would I feel
more virtuous? Who would it benefit?
Discuss for as long as possible …
at least until it gets too dark to see
dust or duster.

27.2.06

Night Train

The last mail train
has clattered into history
along with the poetry.
No more nights of sorting
Auntie Millie's postal order
and Grandma's knitting patterns
whilst clattering past sleeping towns
to arrive on time
for breakfast deliveries.
Once the train would have
been steam: cosy enough
to warm kippers and kedgeree.
Now... romantic as cold tea
mail goes in lorries
jamming up grey motorways,
arriving too late to accompany
hasty bowls of muesli.

25.1.04

Tim's footnote: the poetry referred to in line 3 is probably WH Auden's famous poem 'Night Mail'

Diamonds

Frost sparkles in sunlight:
dazzling diamonds at my feet.
Sweet cold air blows away sleep.
The sky is a blue benediction:
bright as a new birth.

1.2.10

Bare Feet (acrostic)

Beach of great
archaeological importance
revealing Neolithic
evidence:
footprints walking into
eternity,
exploring
their future and our past - together.

17.5.03

Dinner Party

Smiles cut the air, sharp as the crystal:
glasses at attention,
porcelain on parade.

Long table stretches filling the vacuum:
conversation censored,
trivia only.

Dangling earrings reflecting
dazzle from the chandeliers,
our hostess beams, serves
elaborate hors d'oeuvres.

Hours of preparation
apparent in her twitch,
tiny but tangible.

Nervous saliva
dissolves our prime steak. Dessert is a flirt
with cholesterol.

Coffee curdles in the cups.
Chocolates circulate.
Carriages at 12.

7.4.05

Direct Line to Hell

It's music but not as I know it.

Cruel cacophony creeps -

into the darkest parts of my brain.

Horrible pictures form as if drawn by devils.

They evaporate as I switch off the radio,

corpses sucked back into the vacuum.

I hope they'll stay there,

for a long time.

25.1.09

Dolls House

It's a compact dwelling:
one up, one down,
net curtains at the windows,
the outside walls a rose brick pattern.
In the kitchen
an old metal stove
tries to warm up the guests
who perch stiff-necked
on their chairs,
hoping for something nourishing
to appear on the plastic plates.
Upstairs Little Boy Blue sleeps
while his sister plays
with a lazy lead cat
on the mat.
They miss their mother
whose apron and headscarf
stood stiff and starchy
while her thin china arms drooped
below her sleeves,
resigned to the endless round of dusting.
She disappeared one day,
her loss irreplaceable.

28.5.08

'Don't Look back'

Guides appeared in deepest black,
Victorian undertakers puppet-like.
Should we have worn black
on our journey?
Flowers dropped on the glass roof - our grave.
Then, driven by a grim-faced chauffeur to
the empty house, left to
wander in its rooms: we were lost
souls among the dreamy particles
of dust. We saw visions: sleepers not
to be disturbed, vanishing brides,
a room ablaze with candles,
eerie music, film of boatmen
ferrying the dead to the underworld.
It felt peaceful to be dead. Heaps of
obituaries littered the floor like confetti,
snow fell on a model landscape of bare trees
and a church, bridal couple on its roof,
coffin in the distance.

Back in the car I looked at the world of the living
as if at a film.

So death has no fears.   17.5.03

Tim's footnote: Don't Look Back was a site-specific performance by
DreamThinkSpeak at Stanmer House, part of the 2003 Brighton Festival

Dreaming of

Dreaming of ghosts again
I see my brother - younger, healthier
than when he died two years ago.
He smiles assurances and I feel glad
he's all right now. I hold my mother's arm
and steer her through a crowd of relatives
twittering greetings and remembrances.

Alone at home the action turns bizarre:
I'm walking down the stairs with dirty washing
but straight in front of me stands Princess Di.
I hide the grubby underwear and stare
into her once-familiar media face.
Her smile turns nasty and her features darken.
I back away and turn another corner,
convinced she will not follow me so far.

But there she is more frightening than before.
I seize her leg - thinking it will be air
and reassure me there is no-one there.
But solid flesh presses my twitching hands.
I wish I could wake up ...

28.5.08

Faces

I can't face faces in the morning.
The blur of semi-recognition strains
my waking brain. I know that man
enough to say hallo to: "Lovely day!"
And her I know by sight to nod and smile to.
Sometimes half-grimaces are mutual.
We're careful not to hold the eyes too long.
Quick, drop the contact so the stare won't stick,
each scared to be the last to break away.

The stranger's face is easiest to see
float by in seas of anonymity.
But here's a face I've seen before somewhere.
I can't recall the context so I grin
in sheepish non-committal half-aside…
just as I notice her face do the same.
I'm out of context. She can't slot me in.
We scuttle off with noses to the pavement,
safe in our personal, drowsy reveries.

27.9.00

It's not your fault

It's not your fault that the sun won't shine
and the rain fills buckets with tears not wine.

It's not your fault that Tony Blair
pollutes our local Brighton air
with conference noise and windy fuss.
Long will he reign over us.

It's not your fault that babies cry,
that people always tend to die,
that coughing woke me in the night,
that in the morning I'm a fright.

It's not your fault - you can't explain.
Just tell us who we ought to blame.

26.9.00

Dusk (acrostic)

Daylight dies
unafraid of
shadows'
kind embrace.

Twilight (acrostic)

Take a
word that
is ancient but
lovely.
It is
going to be the
highlight of
the day if you let it.

19.1.04

Tim's footnote: it took me a while to spot the hidden rhyme and its wordplay

Blossom in January

It shakes gently in the breeze,
defiant of the season,
a delicious delicate pink
like raspberry ice cream
laid out too early
for a party.

Dream (two haiku)

I held a baby,
felt its weight and milky warmth
but then it was gone.

Dreams fragile as lace,
posing as reality,
deceive, fade and die.

19.1.04

Dust (acrostic)

Dirty particles floating
under the limp duster
scorn its feeble attempts
to annihilate them.

Dust

It's not the fate I would choose
for this body of mine.
Even if it's only a temporary home
for my soul, we've grown quite
attached over the years.
I hate to think of it crumbling
while I float idly in the clouds.
It smacks of bad house-keeping.

6.9.04

Our German Cousin Pedro Says ...

"Slowly, slowly, you have time
to take a shower, change,
gulp down a cool drink,
before we go out to eat."

In a pavement cafe,
taking in the warm air
of a Berlin August evening:
do not rush the experience.
Feel the city's pulse
throbbing gently as we
guess what to eat
from the vast gothic-script menu.
Listen to the rattle of the trams
and the sound of feet on cobbles.
Climb the stone steps back to our
apartment and dream of lakes
lapping at the window.
They are only a dusty
neighbourhood walk away.

6.9.04

Dusting the Dead

My duster rubs their faces
like Aladdin with his lamp.
But there's no magic here.
The dead are just pictures
behind glass, reflections from
the past's great mirror.

21.3.10

Trick of the light

My father woke and saw her…
younger, dark haired
with streaks of grey.
She stood smiling in a red dress.
He was not afraid …
so happy to see her.
When he called the carer
my mother faded away.

He doesn't believe in ghosts.

21.3.10

Not the End

This collection of poems is taken from less than a quarter of the 400 files in Claire's 'Poems' computer folder. Inevitably, the selection reflects my idea of how best to remember Claire and hold her spirit close – you would have to read every poem to get the full view. But I believe the poems in this book tell us much of what it meant to be Claire and to know her, and to help us remember and understand her talents, her fears and hopes, and her loving, joyous and very determined grip on life.

Despite her enduring unhappiness with much of her education, and an often uneasy relationship with her mother, Claire at all times held a deep and resolute faith in life's purpose. There is little in life we can be certain of, but the fate of our material bodies is a given which these poems light on here and there. Meanwhile, the human spirit – like 'soul' and 'consciousness' – is an idea that slips through our busy fingers as inexorably as time itself: yet Claire's poetry catches much of that precious substance too, for there are real depths in her work. The cosmos is a mysterious place – who can say what role love, suffering and happiness ultimately have to play? I remember a little song my mother used to sing as, drawing back the curtains, she filled my bedroom with sunlight: "Good morning, good morning, it's time to say 'Hallo!'; Good morning, good morning, to you!". Sometimes, even at moments of great sorrow, it can feel as if the universe's hands are at work inside us, drawing curtains a little apart to let in a glint of light. At other times those curtains remain tight closed. Maybe one day they will be flung wide and we will be with our loved ones again. Who knows?

Whatever the ultimate fate of anyone's individual humanity, Claire's life and spirit shine on through everyone who knew her – as indeed their love and friendship shone through her while she lived. I personally owe her so much – of happiness, memory, and richness of thought and feeling. And I hope I managed to bring something approaching that wealth of love to her. When it comes to writing though, it is always easier to speak of what is new, or what is missing, or what it is that makes us angry. It is seldom one can stand right back and put into words those things in our life that are constant and seemingly immutable, no matter how much one's happiness depends on them. At least, I like to think that that's why I rarely appear in these poems (no, that's not me in 'Couch Potato' – I don't eat crisps at home!). I felt honoured therefore, and so very pleased, to find, in one poem at least, a truly warm mention of our life together. I leave the careful reader to spot the reference for themselves.

So this is not the end. There are more poems, more memories, and, in countless other surprising and enriching ways, simply more Claire. Somehow, I think there always will be.

Tim, March 2021

Printed in Great Britain
by Amazon

65591947R00076